To Bryan

from

Gary Ju

July 7 2001

AGAINST ALL HAZARDS

Poems of the Peninsular War

AGAINST ALL HAZARDS

Poems of the Peninsular War

by

Harry Turner

Introduction by Ian Fletcher

SPELLMOUNT
Staplehurst

British Library Cataloguing in Publication Data:

A catalogue record for this book is available
from the British Library

Copyright © Harry Turner 2001
Introduction © Ian Fletcher 2001
Map © Spellmount Limited 2001

ISBN 1-86227-133-X

First published in the UK in 2001 by
Spellmount Limited
The Old Rectory
Staplehurst
Kent TN12 OAZ

Tel: 01580 893730
Fax: 01580 893731
E-mail: enquiries@spellmount.com
Website: www.spellmount.com

1 3 5 7 9 8 6 4 2

The right of Harry Turner to be identified
as the author of this work has been asserted by him
in accordance with the Copyright, Designs
and Patents Act 1988

Typeset in Palatino by MATS, Southend-on-Sea, Essex
Printed in Great Britain by
TJ International Ltd, Padstow, Cornwall

Contents

This book is dedicated
to British soldiers of
all ranks past, present
and future.

Introduction

By Ian Fletcher

On 16 May 1811 Colonel William Inglis of the 57th (West Middlesex) Regiment lay wounded on the bloody field of Albuera, while around him his regiment was being decimated by the incessant, murderous, close quarter firing from French infantry of Gazan's 5th Corps. As he lay there, refusing to be carried from the field, he cried out to his men, straining to be heard above the roar of battle: 'Die hard, men! Die hard.' And so they did, until by the end of the day's fighting few of those who marched out that same morning returned to tell the tale. Their sacrifice was not in vain, however, for the day resulted in victory for the Allies, but at a terrible price.

One hundred and eighty-nine years later, on 16 May 2000, I was present at the commemorative events that take place in the village each year on the anniversary of the battle. I was there guiding a party of British visitors around the battlefield and we stood beneath the broiling sun, recalling the tremendously bloody battle that raged on the slopes that today look so peaceful. As we stood there the atmosphere became increasingly heavy and the skies darker, whilst thunder boomed in the distance. Fortunately, we were spared the sort of deluge of rain that proved so fatal to Colborne's brigade on that fateful day in 1811, but the conditions did, nevertheless, bring us closer to the men of Albuera who 'reeled and staggered like sinking ships'. Indeed, William Napier, the great historian of the war, wrote, 'Nothing could stop that astonishing infantry', and as we stood on the very ground across which the Fusilier Brigade made its famous advance, we could almost see them as they cleared the way of

Frenchmen before standing 'triumphant on that fatal hill'.

It was a memorable and moving experience. In fact, so moved was one of my guests, Harry Turner, that, unable to rid his mind of the vivid images that had danced before him that day, he spent the night writing a poem, 'The Slopes of Albuera'. The following morning Harry read the poem to his fellow guests as we stood on the ramparts of the Portuguese fortress of Almeida, itself a silent witness to former great events between 1808 and 1814, the years that mark the beginning and end of the British campaign in the Iberian Peninsula. When he returned home from the trip, Harry was inspired to write more poems, which have been collected in this most enjoyable book, *Against All Hazards*.

The Peninsular War spawned a wealth of literature in the form of memoirs, diaries and letters but, unlike later wars, such as the Great War of 1914–18, it never produced what we might now call 'war poets'. Harry Turner's poems are from the Rudyard Kipling school, rather than the 1914–18 school, and reflect the battles, sieges, and day-to-day existence of Wellington's men. There is no pretentious message, no anti-war sentiment, no criticism of generals, nor any religious slant. They are simply a memorial to all those British soldiers who gave everything for King and Country between 1808 and 1814.

The poems have been arranged chronologically beginning with 'The Convention of Cintra' and ending with 'Last Memories'. The former poem recalls the infamous convention that followed the first battles of the war on 17 and 21 August 1808, at Rolica and Vimeiro respectively. Following the latter action, Sir Arthur Wellesley, as Wellington was still known then, pinned the French against the Lisbon peninsula, forcing them to sue for an armistice. The subsequent agreement allowed the French to sail home in the ships of the Royal Navy. The outcry was tremendous and the three British signatories to the convention, Sir Harry Burrard, Sir Hew Dalrymple and Wellesley himself, were recalled to face a court of inquiry. Fortunately, Wellesley was exonerated of all blame and in April 1809 he returned to Portugal.

Meanwhile, the British Army continued to fight on under

the command of Sir John Moore, who led his men throughout the terrible retreat of the winter of 1808–9. The retreat culminated in a British victory at Corunna on 16 January 1809, but it was a victory that cost Moore his life for he was mortally wounded during the fighting.

Wellesley returned to Portugal in April 1809, and the following month threw the French out of the country following his daring operation to cross the Douro at Oporto. Following this he marched south to join the Spaniards under Cuesta. The two armies linked up at Talavera where, on 27 and 28 July, they defeated the French under Marshal Victor. Two months after the battle the British government saw fit to award Wellesley an earldom, and with it a new name, Wellington.

The following fourteen months saw Wellington's army sitting on the Spanish–Portuguese border in anticipation of the third French invasion. When the French, under Marshal Masséna, finally invaded in late August 1810, they were first delayed at Busaco, where Wellington turned to fight on 27 September 1810, and then, finally, by the famous Lines of Torres Vedras, a series of natural and man-made obstacles north of Lisbon that extended between the Atlantic and the Tagus river.

Masséna and his men sat down before the Lines for five months, until in March 1811 they began their terrible retreat back to Spain, an episode marked by a series of small engagements which culminated in a severe fight at Sabugal on 4 April. The third and last French invasion had ended in failure.

The two main battles of 1811 came at Fuentes de Oñoro on 3–5 May, and at Albuera on 16 May. Both ended in victories for the Allies but they were close-run affairs, particularly Albuera. It was a bloody battle and the casualties horrendous on both sides. It was also the battle that inspired the poems in this book.

In January 1812 Wellington snatched Ciudad Rodrigo from the French and two months later returned to lay siege to Badajoz, a town which had denied them the previous year and which was hated by the British soldiers. There was a score to settle here and it was settled in gloriously bloody style when, on the terrible night of 6 April, Wellington's men wrenched it from the French after a series of brutally spectacular assaults. After the storming, the battle-crazed British went berserk and embarked upon a seventy-two-hour orgy of rape and pillage.

Wellington's army staggered away from Badajoz and marched north, back towards Ciudad Rodrigo. In June they were on the march again towards Salamanca and there, on 22 July, Wellington struck and destroyed the French under Marshal Marmont. It was a crushing victory that opened the way to Madrid, Wellington entering the Spanish capital on 12 August. Despite the successes of 1812 the year ended in disappointment following Wellington's failure at Burgos, an episode that resulted in the infamous retreat that ended back on the Portuguese border. It was Wellington's one and only failure of the Peninsular War.

The decisive year of the war was 1813. The campaigning began in May with Wellington's advance into Spain. His army had recovered from the rigours of the retreat from Burgos, and on 21 June his forces converged upon Vitoria where he smashed the armies of King Joseph to put an end to French aspirations in the Peninsula once and for all.

From Vitoria the road led to the Pyrenees where Wellington left the fighting to his lieutenants. The battle for the passes in July was desperate and almost resulted in victory for the French, whose objective was the relief of Pamplona. Unfortunately for them, Wellington intervened to thwart them at Sorauren, after which he flung them back across the Pyrenees for good.

On 31 August the fortress of San Sebastian fell to the Allies, leaving Wellington to contemplate the invasion of France, which duly took place on 7 October. The French retreated to their positions atop the low range of hills along the river Nivelle and here, on 10 November 1813, Wellington achieved one of his greatest victories. The French hoped their redoubts would stop Wellington but, as the historian of the war, Napier, wrote, 'He tore down Soult's iron barrier as if it were a screen of reeds.'

By now Wellington had both feet planted firmly upon the

'sacred soil' of Napoleon's France. French resistance was feeble and even Soult's counter-attack of 9–13 December at the Battle of the Nive failed to shift the Allies. Indeed, by early 1814 Soult was in retreat away from Bayonne, heading east towards Toulouse. On 27 February Wellington caught up with him and defeated him at the Battle of Orthes, and on 10 April he brought the war to a successful conclusion with the Battle of Toulouse, a bloody affair that ended unsatisfactorily for Wellington.

Although neither side knew it, Napoleon had abdicated on 6 April, so the final battle of the war need never have been fought. The Peninsular War was over, but there still remained one final tragedy to be played out, for on the night of 14 April General Thouvenot, the governor of Bayonne, decided to launch a sortie which resulted in over 1,500 casualties for both sides. It was a needless and pointless action.

Harry Turner's poems reflect the trials and tribulations of Wellington's men during the six-year campaign in the Peninsula. The poetry has been inspired by visits to the old haunts of Wellington's men, the battlefields, and the nondescript towns and villages of many a Spanish and Portuguese backwater. They are also inspired by the numerous memoirs and diaries of those who fought in the Peninsula, men like William Wheeler and William Napier, both of whom are mentioned in this book. They also recall the role of the Spanish guerrillas, of the women who followed the drum, the rations and the quarters, and the battles and sieges that were fought, all of which was done 'Against all Hazards'. Enjoy the poetry.

Ian Fletcher
Rochester, 2001

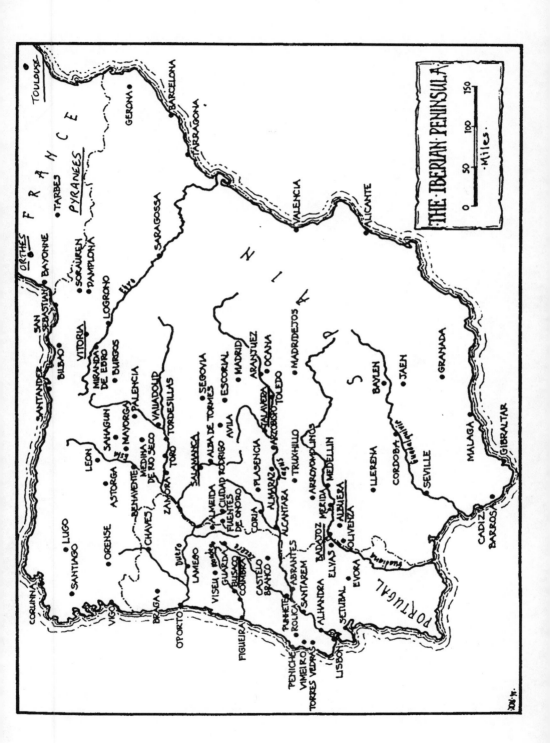

XV

Author's Note

I am grateful to the following sources which afforded me much inspiration when writing the poems.

Bruce, Evangeline, *Napoleon and Josephine*, London: Weidenfeld & Nicolson, 1995

Fletcher, Ian, *Wellington's Regiments*, Staplehurst: Spellmount, 1994

Glover, Michael, *Peninsular Victories*, Gloucester: Windrush Press, 1963

Guedalla, Philip, *The Duke*, London: Wordsworth Editions, 1997

Hibbert, Christopher, *Wellington. A Personal History*, London: HarperCollins, 1997

Le Marchant, Denis, *Memoirs of the Late Major-General Le Marchant*, Staplehurst: Spellmount, 1997

Longford, Elizabeth, *Years of the Sword*, London: Weidenfeld & Nicolson, 1969

Maxwell, W H, *Life of the Duke of Wellington*, London: Henry Bohn, 1852

Stanhope, Lord, *Conversations with Wellington*, London: Prion, 1998

Weller, Jac, *Wellington in the Peninsula*, London: Greenhill Books, 1999

and, above all, Ian Fletcher's brilliant account of the Siege of Badajoz, *In Hell Before Daylight* (Staplehurst: Spellmount, 1984).

I am also grateful to the staff of Apsley House, London and Stratfield Saye for their courtesy and patience with my many questions.

Any errors or omissions are mine entirely, although I have tried throughout to maintain historical, military and geographical accuracy.

Harry Turner
Deepcut, Surrey, 2001

The Poems

1

THE SOLDIER'S LAMENT

Now I was born near Spitalfields,
A costermonger's son,
Yet 'ere I sit in blisterin' heat
Holding a blooming gun.

It's funny when you think on it
What makes the old world run.
Instead of eatin' jellied eels,
I'm stuck wiv currant bun.

No matter though – I won't complain,
There's others worse 'n me.
Just yesterday a mate of mine,
Got a ball right through 'is knee.

An others too did even worse,
Like Jack and Pete and Fred.
It's hard to get to grips wiv it,
Acceptin' that they're dead.

And they was young, no more than boys,
All three, a bunch of chancers.
But then, God's truth, their luck run out,
When they met those Polish Lancers.

I saw 'em there, just lying still,
Their tunics torn and tattered,
Their faces turned up to the sun,
Their bodies pierced and battered.

I tried to cry, me eyes were dry.
Me throat was tight and chokin'.
And yet today – what can I say –
Those still alive are jokin'.

Me boots are worn, me trousers stink,
The skin on me face is peelin'.
Surrounded now by blood and death,
Perhaps I'm losin' feelin'.

We're waiting for the food to come,
If it's meat we'll be darn lucky.
A mate o' mine ate cat today,
Now that's what I call plucky.

An' all around dead soldiers lie,
We 'aint had time to bury.
They're swellin' up in the noonday heat.
It's a sight that's far from merry.

At times like this you fink of 'ome,
Of beer and girls and stuff.
That barmaid at the Tavern Green
You used to fink was rough.

My ma was ill when I left home
And sailed away from blighty.
I dreams of 'er occasionally,
And prays to God Almighty.

But it's no use a'worrying,
'Cos we're 'ere to do some killin'.
Oh yes we are – and that's the deal
When you take the old King's shillin'.

An officer come up to me just now,
'Is uniform was stinkin'.
His epaulettes were 'anging off
As if he'd been out drinkin'.

But 'e was young, as young as me,
I doubt if 'e was twenty.
And somethin' in his cold blue eyes,
Suggested 'e'd had plenty.

But then I saw his tunic gape
And there right on his breast,
The biggest wound you've ever seen,
Compared to all the rest.

The cut was deep and bleedin' fast,
Then the officer fell over.
He lay quite still, as dead men will,
A boy among the clover.

I closed 'is eyes and touched 'is face,
It was warm and sort of restful,
And he was gone, yet hours ago,
His fightin' 'ad been zestful.

And when we're dead, we're all the same,
'Aint nothin' there distinguished.
General or private, make no odds
When life has been extinguished.

But I'm still 'ere and by tonight
I'll have food in my belly.
By the break of day, when the bugles play,
We'll follow old Lord Welly.

Over the hills and far away,
We'll continue with the battle.
Through the fires of hell, we know damn well,
We won't stop till death's last rattle.

2

THE CONVENTION OF CINTRA

O fateful document of shame,
Who in the end will history blame?
Signed at the time – it all seemed simple,
At least to Burrard* and Dalrymple*.

But they were quite old,
And their outlook was insular,
Unschooled in the ways
Of the Lisbon Peninsula.

French Marshal Junot was caught in a trap,
His troops blocked in Lisbon
Faced certain mishap.

What appealed to the British, was clearly they'd won
Without firing once, from cannon or gun,
So they let the French go, with their ill-gotten plunder
And in British ships too, now was this a blunder?

Called back to England to censure and scorn,
The two ancient Generals looked tired and forlorn,
And with them was Wellesley, still young and frustrated,
A subordinate too – a position he hated.

The Court of Inquiry examined all three,
And published their verdict for England to see.
Young Wellesley was cleared and he smiled once again,
And was sent back – Commander of the forces in Spain.

* Sir Harry Burrard and Sir Hew Dalrymple, two elderly Officers who
were placed over Wellesley in 1808 to command British forces in the
Iberian Peninsula.

3

CORUNNA LAMENT

Where sprays of surf and foam-tipped waves
Lap the foreshore churned and serried,
Below an ancient citadel
Is where John Moore is buried.

On high ground by the ramparts,
Close to the place he died,
Was where he chose his final rest,
By a gallant comrade's* side.

Once blamed for his performance,
As a quitter and a runner,
As the man who fled with British troops
To the sea port of Corunna.

Though many shared this hostile view,
And deemed his tactics reckless,
They overlooked one salient point,
That his allies were quite feckless.

The Spanish were most dilatory,
And very far from blameless,
Occasionally on the battlefield,
They were ineffectually shameless.

Outnumbered by old Marshal Soult,
The British then faced slaughter
By French Dragoons and Cuirassiers,
Who never offered quarter.

* Brigadier-General Anstruther

Soult's massive ranks of infantry,
His cavalry and guns,
The cream of France's soldiery,
The Empire's bravest sons.

Thus face to face with tragedy,
Destruction and defeat,
Sir John had little option left,
Except to sound retreat.

The mountains of Galicia,
Inhospitable and bleak,
Were the only real escape route
That Sir John was forced to seek.

In weather most appalling,
With foodstuffs running low,
The British made that journey,
They had many miles to go.*

At last they reached Corunna,
And turned to face the foe,
Behind them lay the ocean,
There was nowhere else to go.

We all know how they fought there,
They couldn't run or hide.
Against all odds they struggled
To save their country's pride.

And thus they did repulse the French
And gave them a hard pounding,
But victory was dearly bought,
The cost of life astounding.

* 250 miles

At length with smoke and cannon-fire
Still roaring in their skulls,
The British began boarding ships,
Packing wounded in their hulls.

Behind them on the broken turf
As they set sail for Britain,
Sir John lay dying bravely.
He had been severely smitten.

Consider all the critics then
Who damned Sir John's fair name.
Consider too another voice,
Who, far from placing blame,

Instead spoke warmly of the man,
Paid tribute to his skill,
Proclaimed as wrong the carping throng,
Who sought to do him ill.

Who was the man who spoke out thus,
Moore's honour to reclaim?
Just England's most illustrious son,
And Wellington* was his name.

* As an old man at the Horse Guards, Wellington said to the future Lord
Raglan, 'You know, Fitzroy, we'd not have won, I think, without him'.

4

THE EVE OF TALAVERA

The sun was an orb, igniting the sky,
The hillsides were fissured and burning,
And even the rock plants were gasping for life,
And the grasslands for water were yearning.

It was on this terrain, in the heartland of Spain,
That Wellesley planned to meet Cuesta.
Though initially cheerful, Wellesley was fearful,
That their friendship would soon start to fester.

Much had been promised, in the form of supplies,
Spanish packhorses, bullock-carts, food;
But none was delivered, not even a crust,
Thus darkening Wellesley's mood.

And Cuesta himself was a problem,
A proud man of seventy-two,
He seemed unable to grasp the essentials
Of what Spain had promised to do.

So physically weak and unsteady,
And a difficult man to approach,
He needed the help of three soldiers,
Just to lift him up into his coach.

Both obstinate and truculent
And sensitive of his status,
This ancient Spanish officer,
Would trigger a hiatus.

The road to Talavera,
Where the river Tagus runs,
Was a vital point at which
Wellesley mustered up his guns.

At three o'clock that morning,
Under cork and olive trees,
Wellesley's officers were anxious
The initiative to seize.

Cuesta's role was clear and simple,
He would lead the first attack
Across the bridge on the Tagus,
At dawn's first wakening crack.

Then following immediately,
The bulk of Wellesley's men
Would strike the French at flank and rear
And scatter them again.

Thus patiently did Wellesley wait,
As dawn painted light the sky,
But no sound could be heard of the Spanish,
Just a soaring eagle's cry.

After three hours with men at the ready,
All primed up and eager to go,
He wondered if these cunning Frenchmen,
Had now struck a pre-emptive blow.

At length with his patience exhausted,
Sir Arthur re-mounted his horse.
He would ride to the lines of the Spaniards,
To see why his plan was off course.

He arrived at the camp at a gallop,
Uncertain of what he would find.
Had the Spanish been slaughtered while resting?
Was a question that gnawed at his mind.

But still in his tent sleeping deeply,
Unmoved by the bustle outside,
Lay Spain's Captain-General Commanding,
A man of extraordinary pride.

When wakened by Wellesley's presence,
The old man seemed far from perturbed.
As he staggered from bed, he shook his grey head,
As a man does whose sleep's been disturbed.

Wellesley turned to an aide of the Spaniard,
Who lounged on a small wooden bench,
'Pray enquire if you will, why the General is here
And not now engaging the French.'

The question was put to the General,
Who yawned and scratched at his breast,
'My soldiers are too tired for fighting,
So I've ordered them all now to rest'.

Now Wellesley's frustration and anger,
Were clear for the Spanish to see,
If the attack had proceeded correctly,
They'd have triumphed – not long after three.

It's often said, in time of war,
Man's fortunes rise and fall.
And though outnumbered heavily,
The British still walked tall.

Though casualties were heavy,
And Cuesta's role insane,
The thin red lines, as in past times,
Outfought the French again.

The French commander, Victor,
Unfortunately named,
Had fled the field, his fate was sealed,
His reputation stained.

So cheer up you lads and keep marching,
To the beat of your regiment's drum,
For before you get old, or in graves you grow cold,
There's more glory and triumph to come.

5

ENTENTE CORDIALE!

Salute the common soldier,
A drunkard and a brute,
But fêted as a hero
When the cannons start to shoot.

A cynic's observation, with perhaps a ring of truth?
Or just a vicious slander without a shred of proof,
In the taverns of old England you are free to make your
choice.
Do you curse your country's soldiers,
Or simply shout 'rejoice'?

Was Wellington quite accurate,
When he called his soldiers 'scum',
Observing somewhat later,
What 'fine fellows' they'd become?

There are countless first hand records,
Of the lives that soldiers led,
How they suffered deprivation,
How they hungered, how they bled.

Among these oft told stories,
There are some that tear your heart,
Acts of gallantry and sacrifice
In which simple men took part.

On more than one occasion,
When the heat of battle raged,
And French and English soldiers,
Fought like animals uncaged.

There came a pause, a brief respite,
When muskets ceased to roar
And men, exhausted, closed their eyes
As if they'd fight no more.

And then across the muddied field,
Still littered with the dead,
Both French and English soldiers,
Would be meeting head to head.

Some men embraced and others wept,
French soldiers offered wine.
The English gave tobacco,
Though 'twas damp and far from fine.

A young Cuirassier removed his cap
And inside was a pancake,
He offered it to an Englishman,
Who responded with a handshake.

These little acts of comradeship
Continued for a while,
And sweating men drew solace,
From another fellow's smile.

Then just beyond this merry scene,
Was heard a bugle call,
An English trumpeter was seen,
Above a ruined wall.

As if to answer it in kind,
Came a French drum's rapid rattle,
Both sides exchanging final gifts,
Before returning to the battle.

Just brief farewells, goodbye, adieu,
Fellow soldiers I salute you.
It grieves me now to have to say,
Next time we meet, I'll shoot you.

6

FUENTES DE OÑORO

A village built of heavy stone,
Streets serpentine and narrow,
With alleyways scarce wide enough
To accommodate a barrow.

And by these straggling granite walls,
All hewn from rock and boulder,
Two thousand British riflemen
Stood shoulder next to shoulder.

The British troops were here deployed,
Just waiting for Masséna,
This marshal of Italian birth,
To enter their arena.

In spite of several fierce assaults,
Impetuously mounted,
The French battalions, ten of them,
Were most severely routed.

But then they crossed the Don Casas,
The river in the village,
And by sheer weight, and efforts great,
They hoped to kill and pillage.

Colonel Williams and the Sixtieth,
Were forced to higher ground,
Where he re-grouped his fighting troops,
The enemy to pound.

The fighting was ferocious now,
And ebbed and flowed like water,
Both hand-to-hand and street-by-street,
The bayonets showed no quarter.

The cavalry of Cotton*,
With impudence and skill,
Had charged Masséna's heavy guns,
And savaged them at will.

Masséna now grew desperate,
And continued to attack,
Some French troops found themselves – six times,
Repulsed and driven back.

At length the French concluded
They would never win the day,
Two thousand dead and wounded
Was the price they were to pay.

This was Masséna's last command,
He was soon to be replaced,
He'd been savaged by the British Lion,
And well beaten, not disgraced.

In Paris several years had passed,
When the Duke next met Masséna
And said to his swarthy, hirsute foe,
'I've not met resistance keener'.

Admiration then, between these men,
Was fundamentally mutual,
Masséna bowed and then replied,
''Twas your tactics that were fruitful.

'And thus, your Grace – such was the stress
Of that fierce and bloody fight,
You can see that now my thick brown hair
Has turned to snowy white.'

* General Sir Stapleton-Cotton, Commander of the British Cavalry.

7

LONDON

In Horse Guards sits a gentleman,
Behind a large oak table,
His brow is furrowed as he writes,
As fast as he is able.

Occasionally he stops his work,
And takes a pinch of snuff,
And then with thin white fingers,
Adjusts a lacy cuff.

He's something of a dandy,
A Whitehall bureaucrat,
His clothes, his hair, his shoes, his hat
Confirm this simple fact.

In front of him, upon the desk,
Are the instruments of his trade,
An abacus, a sharp quill pen,
All beautifully displayed.

He's just about to re-start work,
When a rapping at the door,
Discomodes this elegant gentleman,
And he can write no more.

A clerk comes in, a humble chap,
With papers tied with ribbon,
Incongruous in that book-lined room
With its collected works of Gibbon.

'Forgive me sir,' the clerk explains,
'I have here a dispatch,
It emanates from Lord Wellington,
The latest in a batch.'

He leaves the papers on the desk,
And begs leave to retire,
He knows that soon the minister
Will find their contents dire.

The minister, for such he is,
Unfolds the first crisp sheet,
The writing is in copperplate,
Distinctive, clear and neat.

Thus 'Gentlemen' the note begins,
'I've noted your request,
My officers have responded,
And they've done their very best.

'We know that we're accountable
For each saddle, tent and bridle,
We've done our sums and will attest
That no man here's been idle.

'We've listed spoons and guns and boots,
And tent poles by the score,
All done, I would respectfully add
With the enemy at our door.

'Every farthing's been accounted for,
Well almost every one,
It's hard to be precise, dear sirs,
Under this Spanish sun.

'Unfortunately, I will confess
Diligent as I am,
I can't account for the sad loss
Of a jar of raspberry jam.

'This item, vital to the war,
To the cavalry was issued
In Portugal a month ago,
My guess that it's been misused.

'This brings me to a crucial point,
Or two – if you'll permit,
I need advice from you, dear sirs,
In Whitehall where you sit.

'Two duties face me here in Spain,
Both equally demanding.
But I can't choose which one to take
As Officer Commanding.

'But this for sure, I can't do both,
So pray give me a clue,
Which one to Whitehall is the most
Compelling of the two?

'The first is simple, clear as day,
And may cause us some pain,
I'm to drive Napoleon and his troops
From Portugal and Spain.

'The other is more difficult,
More dangerous to be sure,
To answer the accountants,
Who sit outside your door.

'And thus, dear sir, respectfully,
Your answer I await,
So I can tell my officers,
Before it is too late.

'In the meantime though, forgive me sir,
Presumptuous though I'm sounding,
I'll give Napoleon again,
A good old British pounding.'

8

THE SLOPES OF ALBUERA

Those rolling slopes lie peaceful now
Under the noonday sun,
And only the sound of bird song
Has replaced the crack of the gun.

And the rich red soil
On which wildflowers bloom
Is the colour of soldiers' blood,
As they died and fell,
In that smoky hell,
Covered in sweat and mud.

Shoulder to shoulder they stood there,
Fusiliers, Die Hards and Buffs,
Mere lads from the counties of England,
To the French, just a gaggle of scruffs.

But the red line stood steady
With guns at the ready,
And no power on earth was to break it,
Not a drum-beating Frenchman, nor his
Fierce Polish henchman
Could penetrate, scatter or shake it.

Yes, those rolling slopes are peaceful now,
Under the noonday sun,
And beneath our feet lies buried.
Many a mother's son.

Let's remember them with heavy hearts,
Tinged with a surge of pride,
For they were English soldiers,
And it was for all of us that they died.

9

FRENEIDA

In Portugal there's a village,
Freneida is its name,
Though relatively undistinguished,
It claims a certain fame
As to this dusty, rural place, a British General came.

For Wellington chose this tranquil spot,
With its church and village square,
To set up his headquarters,
And plan the war from there.

The house was unpretentious,
And very far from grand,
No cobblestones surrounded it,
The square was scattered sand.

And outside by the horses,
A humble sergeant waited,
No glitter, pomp or honour guard,
Just vigilance understated.

Unlike the French headquarters,
With its entourage of men,
Dressed gaudily, like peacocks,
There were never less than ten.

With their shiny, plumed helmets,
That glittered like brass,
And their epaulettes all fringed with gold,
They looked to the casual observer,
Like Legionaires fearless and bold.

For Bonaparte rejoiced in show,
With all its servile fawning.
He was an Emperor after all,
Who thought great days were dawning.

Such flummery was alien,
To Wellington at least,
When he appeared in his frock coat,
He might have been a priest.

The contrast, then, between these men,
Was stark and quite revealing.
Napoleon's regal, haughty style,
Manifestly unappealing.

But Wellington, an aristocrat,
While cool and introspective,
Was resolute in his pursuit
Of England's main objective.

So winning was all, and we could walk tall,
As the British, years later, would sing.
But as history shows, and an old soldier knows,
It was always a damn close run thing.

10

TWO WOMEN

Upon a knoll in Surrey
Sits a lady most serene,
And sunlight filters through the trees
To warm this pleasant scene.

A butterfly in lazy flight,
Its wings a blur of gold,
Alights upon the lady's hand,
Quite lovely to behold.

The insect tarries briefly,
Then lifted by a gust,
Wafts heavenwards dramatically,
In a tiny haze of dust.

The lady lays her parasol
Beside a wicker hamper,
As two young children – rosy-cheeked,
On the greensward start to scamper.

A servant clad in livery
And crimson satin breeches,
Lifts up the hamper's wicker lid
Revealing two plump peaches.

The children shriek with sheer delight,
They're both sweet little creatures,
Just like their elegant mother
With her noble English features.

'Now darlings,' she admonishes,
'Please put that fruit aside,
There's other things to eat my dears
If you just look inside.'

And in the box, all neatly packed,
Are York hams, oyster pies,
And candied fruit and crusty loaves,
And much more else besides.

There's silver plate and china,
And a tablecloth of lace,
And sweet white wine and cordials
To suit the children's taste.

The servant spreads the tablecloth,
Adds plates of Dresden china.
In palaces and stately homes,
There surely is none finer.

And as the children start to eat,
They smile up at their mother,
But then quite unexpectedly,
She experiences a shudder.

A thousand leagues away in Spain,
Beneath a scorching sun,
Her husband, who's a Viscount,
Struggles to load his gun.

Before him on that barren slope
With a hundred corpses rotting,
Two Frenchmen, carrying unsheathed swords,
Approach the Viscount, trotting.

Before he has a chance to load
And raise his musket high,
A sabre cut disables him,
And he falls without a cry.

Then a mounted Polish Lancer,
In his stirrups standing tall,
Kills dead the English nobleman
With a single musket ball.

The rain upon the cobblestones
Has made them shine like glass.
It's a London summer thunderstorm
That very soon will pass.

But sheltering in a doorway,
By a tavern near the docks,
Stand a group of shivering women,
Wearing dirty, ragged frocks.

One younger than the others,
With no shoes upon her feet,
Displays soles both black and calloused,
From walking barefoot in the street.

Her belly's tight and swelling,
As round as any drum,
She tugs another woman's arm,
And begs a tot of rum.

The bottle's passed, she takes a swig,
Her young face creased with pain.
She begs another mouthful,
But her plea is all in vain.

The other women shuffle off,
As a weak sun re-appears,
Leaving the young girl on the step,
Alone with just her tears.

A thousand leagues away in Spain,
Beneath the scorching sun,
A soldier, who's her husband,
Is polishing his gun.

It's his first time out of England,
In the heat and dust and flies,
And he's thinking of his woman,
As the sweat drips in his eyes.

He pauses for reflection,
And emits a weary sigh,
Just as a loud explosion,
Illuminates the sky.

The air is thick with shot and shell,
Smoke billows round his head,
A musketball strikes at his breast,
And then the boy is dead.

In London by the tavern steps,
There's a brilliant flash of lightning,
More rain must fall before the sky
Shows any sign of brightening.

A woman in a ragged dress,
Is standing by the dock,
The rain has drenched her clothing,
As she looks up at the clock.

The chimes are sounding loudly now,
As she counts up to eleven.
But as she does, she somehow knows
Her man has gone to heaven.

11

CIUDAD RODRIGO

The wind like a scimitar fashioned from ice,
The earth frozen and coated with snow,
Above them a fortress forbidding,
Through which Wellington's bravehearts must go.

To cut those deep parallel trenches
In earth as unyielding as stone,
Was a job for Wellington's soldiers,
The infantry, digging alone.

No sappers or miners to help them,
No engineers' tools to assist,
Just muscle and sweat and courage,
As around them the icy wind hissed.

British gunners needed those trenches,
Before the siege could begin.
They would lay low the walls of the fortress,
Through which hundreds of men would pour in.

The cannonade opened two breaches,
It was time to start the attack.
Through rubble and flame, red-coated men came,
And not one of them ever looked back.

First up were the men of the Light,
But in darkness, not easy to fight,
As they scrambled in line, an enormous French mine
Exploded and lit up the night.

But more soldiers followed the slain,
They charged through the breach once again,
Their bloody work done, with bayonet and gun,
They felt triumph, exhaustion and pain.

The men on the ramparts stood steady,
But triumph's sweet taste was now chilled,
For in that fierce fight, in the black of the night,
'Bob' Craufurd, their leader, was killed.

The pride of the Light Division,
'Black Bob' was a hard man it's true.
But he loved with a passion his Regiment,
His King, flag and family too.

As he stood on the glacis exhorting
More effort from all of his boys,
A musket ball struck this great soldier,
And he fell midst the smoke and the noise.

While dying high up on the ramparts,
This hard man made one last request,
'Tell my wife, I'll see her in heaven',
Then he lay back at last, free to rest.

12

THE OFFICERS

Sons of the nobility,
Gentlemen of style,
Born in country houses
With drives up to a mile.

Cossetted by nannies,
Servants by the score,
Couldn't tie their laces
Till the age of twenty-four.

Enj oying education
In ivy-covered schools,
Learned to speak in Latin,
But not to handle tools.

Gloucestershire and Leicestershire,
St James's and The Strand,
Was where you'd find these gilded lads,
The wealthiest in the land.

At Mayfair balls, in ducal halls,
At Lady Wentworth's party,
They'd preen and prance – they laugh and dance,
Their appetites were hearty.

In spite of the advantages,
Of money and position,
Not all of them were very bright
Or blessed with erudition.

The Nigels and the Ruperts,
The Reginalds and Freddies,
Were often thick as two short planks,
Grown men who still loved teddies.

So what to do with these young chaps,
The cream of our society,
To go in trade was out of court,
Perhaps a life of piety?

To join the church, become a priest
Was but a gentle fate,
Or just, perchance, to stay at home,
And manage the estate.

There was another choice to make
If the family had the cash,
And the young man in his early prime
Displayed sufficient dash.

A commission as an officer
Could still be bought for money,
The regiments most fashionable
Drew men like bees to honey.

The colonel of a regiment
At the age of twenty-five?
Young Henry Paget managed this,
And continued to survive.

Became Marquess of Anglesey,
And a brilliant soldier too.
But he was very fortunate,
And his reputation grew.

Some critics of this system,
Believed it should be banned,
And then in House of Commons,
It was vigorously damned.

The famous General Tarleton*
Condemned it out of hand,
And soon he found good men agreed,
Delighted with his stand.

But out in Spain and Portugal,
Two thousand leagues away,
Young men were tested in the field,
Midst battle's noisy fray.

When muskets crack and sabres clang,
And smoke hangs overhead,
High rank and noble lineage
Can't help you when your dead.

So young boys were commissioned,
From soldiers in the ranks,
On merit, skill and aptitude,
Earning the nation's thanks.

But Wellington himself, it's said,
While recognising talent,
Found officers drawn from the ranks,
Fell short of being 'gallant'.

This judgement was a trifle harsh,
As history can show,
There were many brave young officers
Promoted from below.

A high-born wealthy gentleman
Might very well be bad,
A bounder and a bullyboy,
A mountebank or cad.

* In The House of Commons, General Banestre Tarleton said: 'Gold and rank are now the only passport to preferment.'

While yet some lad from Essex,
Or a humble butcher's boy,
Could prove a splendid officer,
And give proud parents joy.

To be offered a commission
By George, the English King,
Was a truly signal honour,
And there was no finer thing.

For a nobleman who purchased his,
Or the soldier just promoted,
Both men could serve with zest and verve,
To their country both devoted.

13
BADAJOZ

On the river Guadiana
Stands a major 'Key of Spain',
A mighty fortress city
That the British ache to gain.

The task thus facing Wellington,
Is daunting to be sure.
He must devastate those ramparts,
And then penetrate its core.

With sturdy men assembled,
All his officers agree
That meticulous preparation
Is the key to victory.

So long before the siege begins,
They must make a thorough check
Of guns and tools and foodstuff,
Every bushel, every peck.

They count shovels and gouges,
Tarpaulins and spades,
And gimblets and handsaws
Of various grades.

Chalk lines and cauldrons,
And forge carts complete,
Plus compasses, greasekegs,
Box rulers (two feet).

Axes and sandbags,
Sledgehammers and nails,
Leather buckets and mallets,
And stout metal pails.

Tents for the officers,
Tents for the troops,
Gunpowder and ballast,
And baskets and hoops.

Several firkins of tallow,
Scaling ladders and joints,
And tools for the miners
With sharp metal points.

With all this equipment
Assembled and stacked,
Trench digging must start
Before any attack.

The hard work commences
As rainfall begins,
And soon scores of soldiers
Are in mud to their shins.

Each spadeful of earth,
In a trice turns to slime,
The men look like golliwogs,
Covered in grime.

While up in the fortress,
The Frenchmen prepare,
They bristle with firepower,
They've plenty to spare.

The general commanding is brimming with zest,
A few like to think he's Napoleon's best,
For General Philippon knows that he faces
A colossal assault as his flag he embraces.

But below those tall ramparts, by night and by day,
The British keep digging, deep trenches to lay,
For Wellington knows that before his assault,
He must pour British cannon at the walls of the fort.

The walls rise up steeply, they're massive and thick,
Constructed of masonry, granite and brick.
'Twixt two mighty bastions runs a huge curtain wall,
And below this a ditch in which men soon will fall.

The cannon fire starts, and round iron balls
Start pounding and smashing against those great walls,
The twenty-four* pounders blast off and recoil,
For Wellington's gunners, it's merciless toil.

Great chunks of heavy masonry
Are cracked and start to fall,
And billowing smoke and musket fire
Form an odorous, hanging pall.

The cannonade intensifies,
Those walls are far from weak,
But a breach of some significance
Is what the British seek.

The French respond ferociously
From high up in the fort,
And in the hail of gunfire
Many British troops are caught.

Inspecting his trenches, Lord Wellington sees
Scores of dying and wounded still in mud to their knees,
He makes a decision, prays to God that he's right,
They must storm the great citadel later that night.

Now Wellington's senior officers
Are seeking volunteers,
Known as the famous 'Forlorn Hope',
The cause of widows' tears.

* Wellington's major siege gun with a nine-foot barrel.

These men will be the first to scale
The crumbling fortress wall,
But most will die in the attempt,
And as heroes they will fall.

And so the order's given, move forward and attack,
No man expects a miracle, but no man there looks back.
The valiant British redcoats, like their ancestors before,
Rush to the breach exultant, hoping through it they will pour.

But scaling ladders are too short,
They scarcely reach the top,
And men are butchered on the rungs,
But still they never stop.

A fusilade of musket balls
And vats of burning pitch,
And sharpened spikes affixed to boards
Are hurled down to the ditch.

Above the roar of cannon fire
Come piercing human groans,
As flying fragments, hot as hell,
Slice flesh and splinter bones.

As bodies fall in ragged heaps
On comrades just below,
They still continue climbing,
To the ramparts they must go.

Using corpses for their footholds,
Dodging sword and bayonet thrust,
The British fight like Dervishes,
Now driven by blood lust.

It's hand to hand and face to face,
For officers and men,
As sabre rings on sabre,
Each has the strength of ten.

A soldier of the Ninety-Fourth,
Has scrambled to the top,
He stumbles on a still-warm corpse,
Half-falls and cannot stop.

A French defender lunges,
And launches an attack,
He stabs the soldier fiercely,
All wounds are in the back.

And then the blade slides through him
Like a hog upon a spit,
He screams and vomits blood and foam,
And collapses in the pit.

The slaughter is prodigious,
The ditches clogged with dead,
And with the blood of wounded men,
The walls are painted red.

Thus forty times courageous men
Are hurled into the breach,
But most are skewered, clubbed or shot,
'Ere the ramparts they can reach.

Now Picton* and the glorious Third
Will escalade in vain.
Each time they struggle to the top,
They're driven down again.

At last, with Picton wounded,
Those stalwarts find success
By seizing an embrasure,
Their advantage they can press.

* Commanding the Third Division.

53

The fighting now intensifies,
The death roll escalates,
And Phillipon's defenders
Surround the inner gates.

So many acts of courage,
Such selfless pluck and guts,
Both sides seem quite impervious
To a thousand sabre cuts.

But thus enraged and vengeful,
Five score of British men,
Gain access to the castle wall
And storm it once again.

The breaches won, the ramparts gained,
The castle tower is beckoning,
And from it flies the Frenchmen's flag,
Which soon will face a reckoning.

Young Officer MacPherson,
Though wounded in the chest,
Espies the fluttering standard,
And resolves to do his best.

He scrambles to the tower,
Finds a sentry at his post,
Holds a sabre to the Frenchman's throat
Whose face is like a ghost.

In French he asks the sentry
How he can reach the flag,
The Frenchman shrugs, as Frenchmen do,
But his resistance starts to sag.

And soon this brave defender
Is hustled to one side,
He's only trying to protect
His symbol of French pride.

Macpherson's standing at the top,
The French flag he must seize,
But he has nothing to replace it with
As it billows in the breeze.

Impromptu then, this gallant man,
Decides to improvise,
He tears the old French standard down,
And it no longer flies.

He swiftly takes his jacket off,
His coat of British red,
And runs it up the flagpole
So it will serve instead.

Meantime outside the fortress walls
Upon a barren slope,
Stands Wellington observing,
'Is this a forlorn hope?'

Reports are not encouraging,
So many men lie dead,
And victory seems elusive
With more carnage just ahead.

He stands there like a statue,
Lit by a torch's glare,
As before him in the breaches,
Cannons and muskets flare.

As he contemplates withdrawal,
A young officer appears,
A messenger with more bad news
Is what Wellington now fears.

But far from bad, the news is good,
The castle has been taken
By Picton and the glorious Third,
The French are deeply shaken.

Now Wellington's face lights up
As he turns toward the breaches,
'The place is ours,' he now exclaims,
As for his sword he reaches.

But there's still bloody work to do,
More men must die in dozens,
Old and young, father and son,
Nephews, brothers, cousins.

At last the French are beaten,
Though bravely they have fought,
And Wellington's great triumph,
Has been very dearly bought.

But what follows this engagement
Besmirches England's name,
As the behaviour of our soldiers,
Is the cause of national shame.

Murder, rape and looting,
Acts of savagery, abhorrent,
Drunken men cavort like animals
In a raging mindless torrent.

They've won a bloody battle,
Lost comrades by the score,
And now their lust for vengeance
Sees them smash down every door.

No persons are respected,
Not artisan or nun,
The rich man and the beggar,
Are subjected to the gun.

Men fire through doors and windows,
And even at church bells,
And citizens of ancient years,
Are put through seven hells.

All human sense abandoned,
All pity cast aside,
Just a burning lust for plunder,
No shame nor hint of pride.

And casks of wine are opened,
And flow around their feet,
As soldiers tear their tunics off,
And lurch along the street,

The fury and destruction,
Will eventually subside,
With officers incapable
Of stemming this wild tide.

A gallows is erected,
A warning grim and stark,
But no man's hanged, it is too late
On vengeance to embark.

So thus it is a victory,
With dead men by the score,
But history will not wipe clean,
This blemish on the war.

As Wellington, grim visaged,
Surveys his butchered dead,
For the first time on the battlefield,
He weeps for those he's led.

'The capture of Badajoz affords as strong an instance of the gallantry of
our troops as has ever been displayed. But I anxiously hope that I shall
never again be the instrument of putting them to such a test as that to
which they were put last night.'

Wellington in his letter to Prime Minister Lord Liverpool.

14

FORT CONCEPCIÓN

Those mighty walls like broken teeth
Are open to the skies,
And crumbling slabs with lichen hung,
Echo with ghostly sighs.

The glacis and escarpments,
The ramparts and redoubts,
Though empty now and ruined,
Once rang with soldiers' shouts.

It seems like a cathedral now,
Though once a place of war,
Where kegs of powder, musket balls
Were piled and kept in store.

The cobbles and the flagstones
Are choked with grass and thistle.
No more the stamp of soldiers' boots
Or a sergeant's piercing whistle.

At night when all is darkness
And nocturnal owls are hooting,
You will hear the sound, quite faintly,
Of ghost soldiers practise shooting.

And if you stand quite motionless,
On the massive granite walls,
You can smell the scent of horses
And imagine bugle calls.

There's something deep and timeless
Locked in this ruined place,
As if the very stones themselves
Have absorbed a kind of grace.

Redolent with memories,
That drift down through the years,
Fort Concepción is a shrine-like place,
That's been washed by English tears.

15

HARD RATIONS

Salute the humble maggot,
He's a horrid, wriggly fellow,
He lives in army biscuits,
And his colour is bright yellow.

But common soldiers ain't concerned
When their bellies start to rumble,
So let Napier* sneer, and others jeer,
For starving men don't grumble.

* Charles Napier wrote: 'We are on biscuits full of maggots and though
not a bad soldier, hang me if I can relish maggots.'

16

THE SENTRY BOY

In the velvet, purple darkness,
Where no stars shine overhead,
Every night sound, every rustle,
Magnifies nocturnal dread.

Sitting with your Baker rifle
Slung across your nervous knees,
Peering down that inky hillside
At the twisted olive trees.

Hear your heartbeats loudly drumming,
Feel the sweat upon your face.
When will dawn arrive – if ever
In this bleak and lonely place?

Now your empty belly's churning,
Haven't eaten for a week,
Save for scraps of rancid rabbit,
Touch the hollows of your cheek.

Swollen feet and blistered fingers,
Aching bones and weary eye,
Staring at the blurry skyline
Where tomorrow men will die.

God forsaken, hope abandoned,
Is this the place your life will cease?
Riddled by a hail of bullets,
Only death can bring release.

Think of sweethearts, think of mother,
Concentrate on other things,
Try and bottle down your terror,
Though it flies on silent wings.

You're a soldier and a hero,
Destined for a noble death.
But what was that? is something stirring?
Grip your rifle, hold your breath.

No, it's nothing, just a phantom,
Wind among the olive trees,
Getting jumpy, must control it,
Or the sergeant won't be pleased.

If you see a foreign soldier
Creeping forward in the dark,
Your instructions are to shoot him,
Kill him dead and make your mark.

But suppose that he's a young 'un,
Under twenty he might be,
Can you snuff him like a candle
Flickering on a Christmas tree?

Dawn is coming, soft and ghostly,
Creeping over hedge and hill,
Soon the Spanish sun will blossom,
Burning off the cold night's chill.

Back beyond you hear a bugle,
Rousing men from dreamless sleep,
Horses coughing, neighing, stamping,
Yet you must your vigil keep.

No respite until you're ordered,
Can't abandon post or gun,
You must wait for your replacement,
Thanks to God, pray soon he'll come.

Now the sun has risen swiftly,
Bathing you in yellow light,
Glinting on your belt and buckles,
Melting fears you felt at night.

Now you stand and look before you,
Marvel at those fields so green,
For today it is your birthday,
And your age is seventeen.

17

SALAMANCA

A city stirs from fitful sleep,
Its date with destiny to keep,
Beyond its castellated walls,
A muted trumpet softly calls.

'To arms! to arms!' it seems to say,
'Unsheath your swords without delay',
And soldiers rise, and stamp and groan,
They're many, many miles from home.

Some, as they pull their jackets tight,
Still groggy from the dreams of night,
Have not a button left to show,
For all have been removed, and lo!

Just beaten flat to discs that make
A most amazing kind of fake,
Passed off as English coin most fine,
And used to purchase Spanish wine.

But trivial things that soldiers do
Are now forgot, as soon they view
The French arrayed in fiercesome force,
With musket, cannon, prancing horse.

Out on the dusty, dawn-kissed plain,
The generals scan the bleak terrain,
The French have massed upon the hill,
Known as the Greater Arapil.

And as the skirmishing begins,
Both armies know that who dares wins.
French Marshal Marmont, through his glass,
Sees dust rise up as soldiers pass.

But it's the dust of a baggage train,
Deceived, old Marmont looks again,
'The English army moves in mass!'
But he is wrong, his judgement crass.

Contriving now to strike and win,
He gathers all his generals in.
His plan is simple, quick and deft,
Let Thomières move to the left.

This leftward movement gathers pace,
The general quickly creates space,
But it's too wide, a yawning gap,
Has Frenchie set himself a trap?

While Wellington, a league away,
Is served cold chicken on a tray,
To him it matters not a jot,
For aides bring news that's piping hot.

The French are in motion
With muskets held high,
'Observe what they're doing'
Is the great man's reply.

'They move to the left, their manoeuvring's neat.'
At this news Lord Wellington leaps to his feet,
The half-eaten chicken is tossed in the air,
He seizes his glass from the canvas camp chair.

'The devil they are!' is Lord Wellington's cry,
The glass still fixed firmly to his keen soldier's eye.
'There's a foe who's confused, his judgement is false,
Pray give me my sword sir, and bring up my horse.'

Opportunity beckons, it's the chance that they need,
He springs in the saddle and makes off at speed.
Stretched like a greyhound fresh out of its slip,
He urges his mount on with spurs and the whip.

There's surprise in the ranks, and no little pride
When Wellington canters right up to their side,
'Hold hard the third,' he says halting his steed,
And issues instructions with crispness and speed.

The noble Lord Pakenham's touched on the arm,
He's to 'move up the third', and cause the French harm,
Laconic and haughty, but ready to kill,
His answer to Wellington, 'my Lord I will'.

Now Wellington turns to ride up to the crest,
For observing the battle, high ground is the best.
But while he gives orders, 'increase the attack',
The French, now uncertain, may draw their line back.

Marmont is edgy, his left flank exposed,
Whatever he does, he must get that gap closed.
As he climbs on his horse to sound the alarm,
A shell bursts beside him and smashes his arm.

A general called Bonnet takes over as chief,
But he too is wounded, compounding French grief.
And now the two armies ignite and explode,
The air's pierced with battle cries, 'fire and re-load'.

And thus on it rages with shot and with shell,
As sabre strikes sabre, the music of hell.
Men bleeding and panting, stumble and fall
And disembowelled horses die galloping tall.

As Pakenham's Third are approaching the hill,
The French batteries blast them, firing at will.
The brigade led by Wallace are cut down like wheat
As a torrent of bullets belch flames, smoke and heat.

The Third rallies bravely, no man turns his back
As they re-form their ranks for a counter attack.
Brave Wallace addresses his shattered brigade,
They stand shoulder to shoulder, as if on parade.

The French seem bemused, confused to a man,
Their murderous firepower has not worked to plan.
Their order is broken, most turn on their heel,
And soon those French soldiers will taste British steel.

French General Thomières, brave to the last,
Is finally killed by a fierce musket blast.
The British have routed the enemy force,
Ably assisted by Portuguese horse.

But fighting continues elsewhere on the field,
There's more to be done before all the French yield.
Six guns have been captured and many men slain,
And a gleaming French eagle the allies now claim.

Smoke rises in clouds on the wide open plain
As Wellington's army scents victory again.
There's Leith and there's Bradford and brave D'Urban too,
Von Alten and Bock to name but a few.

All Wellington's off icers
Are tough, proud and bold,
And when they go home,
What tales will be told!

There's others of merit, like Stapleton Cotton,
And the King's German Legion should not be forgotten.
The names of these heroes reach high to the sky,
Like Dowson and Fletcher, Pringle and Spry.

But down in the smoke and the blood and the dead,
There's one more important thing to be said;
The ordinary soldier is gallant and willing,
He fights for his country not just the King's shilling.

And now the French columns retire from their crest,
And form up again, English horses to test.
As French cannon belches more fire from the rear,
A drumbeat is heard, its signal not clear.

French musket fire starts, spurting hot lead and flame,
And Wellington knows he must now raise his game.
He turns to a comrade of legendary fame,
John Gaspard Le Marchant is the Guernseyman's name.

'You must charge at all hazards with sabre and gun,
Those squares must be smashed before battle is won.'
Le Marchant's Dragoons are wheeled into line,
And the 3rd, 4th and 5th wait, intense, for his sign.

The scene that then follows warms every man's heart,
As the huge English horses are straining to start.
The French are re-grouping, but shattered and broken,
When over the ridge bursts a nightmare unspoken.

A thousand men strong,
At a thundering pace,
Holding long, gleaming swords
Is what Frenchie must face.

From acts of raw courage, the Frenchmen don't shirk,
But the sharp Dragoon swords do their terrible work.
Le Marchant's triumphant, he spurs on his steed,
Urging the great horse to maximum speed.

Pursuing the French to the edge of the trees,
He sees a French soldier, ahead on his knees.
But he's holding a musket, and aiming to fire,
Le Marchant reins in, but he cannot retire.

The shot strikes the General
With sickening force,
And slowly, while dying,
He slides from his horse.

The British in triumph
Have made the French yield,
Unaware that a hero
Has been lost in the field.

The French do attempt
A brave counter-attack,
But after more fighting
They're soon driven back.

The day has been won,
And the British flag's flying
Over smoking remains
And the dead and the dying.

And later that evening
As Wellington dreams,
He sees ghosts in his sleep
And hears wounded men's screams.

The night air is still
From the wind, not a breath,
For tomorrow there follows
More bloodshed, more death.

18

GARCIA HERNANDEZ

By this small, dusty town,
In a vast Spanish region,
The legend was born
Of the King's German Legion.

Still stunned from their mauling
The previous day,
The French rearguard columns
Were marching away.

Demoralised soldiers
Bruised, battered and shattered,
Drifted aimlessly round
As if nothing else mattered.

They hoped to escape,
But their hopes were in vain,
For the Allies, pursuing,
Would smite them again.

Lord Wellington, riding ahead with his troop,
Observed Curto's chasseurs
Attempt to re-group.
His instructions to Anson,
The British Dragoon,
Were 'engage the French fiercely',
And 'do it damn soon'.

As Anson's men charged,
Joined by Decken and Bock,
The King's German Legion
Received their first shock.

They were struck by a volley
Of murderous force,
Which sliced through the lines
Of both rider and horse.

The fusilade came
From a massive array
Of the French forming square
In the classical way.

Many saddles were emptied,
As the charge gathered pace,
But the riderless horses
Showed no lack of pace.

Von Der Decken was wounded,
And so was his mare,
But he galloped on forward
Right up to the square.

Thrashing and kicking,
The noble beast fell,
Creating a gap
Through which thundered, pell mell
The heavy Dragoons
With long swords of steel.
They had breached the French square,
And had made the French reel.

No quarter was given,
No quarter was asked,
As the King's German Legion
Completed their task.

In just forty minutes,
Against all the odds,
They'd routed the French
And baffled the gods.

Though battle smoke clears
And corpses will rot,
The deeds done that day
Will not be forgot.

For although years pass by
And allegiances change,
A toast among soldiers
To others seems strange.

So raise up your glasses, lads,
As this story you tell,
And drink to the memory
Of the brave K.G.L.

19

THE SURGEONS

To mangle with impunity,
To hack and amputate
With scalpel, saw and tourniquet,
Curved needle, draining plate.

Thus did the army surgeons,
Their bloody work deploy,
They toiled in foul conditions,
Devoid of thanks or joy.

In stinking tents, on groaning boards,
They worked stripped to their loins,
And more than once a desperate man,
Would bribe them with loose coins.

To save a limb, an eye, a hand,
Was what the bribe was for.
But broken bones and gaping wounds,
Were the wages of this war.

Some men who lay there gasping,
Their life-blood draining fast,
Were stoic, as the surgeons
Kept struggling to the last.

One soldier of the 50th,
Who's name we'll never know,
Ate almonds from his waistcoat
While they hacked and cut below.

His thigh was sawn, through flesh and bone,
But he never made a cry,
He accepted it in silence,
Just grateful not to die.

A corporal named Buchanan,
Had thirteen wounds, it's said,
He also had his nose cut off,
And yet he wasn't dead.

The surgeons staunched his bleeding,
Then stitched the fellow up.
Years later he'd display his wounds
Over a brimming cup.

But surgeons too were heroes,
As about their tasks they set,
No glory would accumulate,
Few medals they would get.

Just thankless work unending,
In heat and bitter cold,
As part of English history,
Their great story must be told.

20

LOS PARTIDAS

No feathered hats, no uniforms
To shield them from the weather,
No long swords from Toledo,
In scabbards of fine leather.

Guerrillas by another name,
Marauders most mischievous,
Bandidos, villains, cut-throat dogs,
Their fieldcraft crude but devious.

Their wanton plunder of supplies,
Interception of dispatches,
Had caused the French as much distress,
As gunpowder touched by matches.

More lethal than the Spanish troops,
In harassing the Frenchman,
And famous for their fickleness
And promiscuous choice of henchman.

They also ravaged British lines,
Causing Wellington frustration,
And showed a flagrant disregard
For their battered Spanish nation.

Were they patriotic heroes then,
As they roamed the Spanish plain?
Or craven opportunists
Causing endless grief and pain.

In that time of bloody conflict,
Triumph, tragedy and pride,
Carrion men cried out for burial
And they came from either side.

Los Partidas were no different,
Good and bad in equal parts,
Some were brave and loved their country,
Others had black, knavish hearts.

Now that years have leavened sorrow,
Softened hatreds keenly felt,
Made the memories of these horrors,
Grow much fainter, even melt.

For all lie deeply buried,
'Neath the sun-baked Spanish sod,
Half-forgotten, half-forgiven,
As they make their peace with God.

SOLDIERS ON A MARCH
To pack up their Tatters and follow the Drum

21

THE CAMP FOLLOWERS

They drift across the open plain,
Like a ragged army troop,
Torn dresses, filthy cloaks,
Many walking with a stoop.

Rum-swilling, sewer breath,
Among the reeking dead,
Stripping corpses with their fingers,
Lice alive in every head.

Huddled by the tethered horses,
Near the campfires rosy glow,
Women in all shapes and sizes,
Sleep exhausted, row by row.

Some are wives of serving soldiers,
Faithful spouses to their men,
Suffering every deprivation,
Yet each dawn they'll march again.

Fiercely loyal to their husbands
And their regiments as well,
Washing, cooking, stealing, scrounging,
Angels in the fires of hell.

Not for them fine silks and perfumes,
Lacy petticoats and frills.
Rotting cotton clothes their bodies,
Exposing them to winter's chills.

And among them, desperate women,
Who amidst all ranks will roam,
Offering their tired bodies
To the soldiers far from home.

Easy now to mock and titter,
Demonise their tawdry fate,
Condemn them as a plague of vultures
Unwelcome at God's pearly gate.

Though one hesitates to name him,
Wellington, it must be said,
Thought them devils quite incarnate,
Had them flogged and wished them dead.

Let this writer now explain,
Though it gives him grievous pain
To state that Wellington was wrong,
Those women were both brave and strong.

Thus through the mist of history's years,
And watered by dead widows' tears,
Let's praise those women, young and old,
Acknowledge when this story's told.

That they were made of sterner stuff,
Magnificent, heroic, tough,
Come! let's remove this wretched stain
That still besmirches their fair name.

It's not too late to make amends,
It matters not whom this offends,
So let us set the record straight,
Those women all – weren't bad – but great.

Just one example will suffice,
About a humble soldier's wife,
Mrs Skiddy was her name,
Her actions brought her modest fame.

Her husband, during a retreat,
Could scarcely stand upon his feet.
This woman took him on her back,
Including musket and knapsack.

Three miles she took the tired man,
Through arid scrubland, mud and sand,
And though no medals did she get,
Let Englishmen please not forget.

That Mrs Skiddy, rough and square,
Should feature in each soldier's prayer,
And to the heavens raise your glass,
Before another day should pass,
Salute the women – every one,
Just like the girl who bore your son.

22

THE GENERALS

Messéna, Marmont, Jourdan and Soult,
Were some of the 'Generals'
Wellington fought,
Though proud and distinguished, stout hearted and keen,
They were not quite a match
For the Duke's British team.

With Craufurd and Picton,
Le Marchant and Hill,
Just a few made subjective
To Wellington's will.

The Marquis of Anglesey
Minus a limb,
And Sir John Hope of Hopetown,
Clean shaven and trim.

For Wellington's Generals
Weren't all just the same.
Bob Craufurd was brilliant
And Beresford – tame.

And Uxbridge, that stalwart,
Though loyal and true,
Was never in truth
The Duke's number two.

If the 'Croakers' today
Wish to still cock a snook,
There's maybe one fair shot
To aim at the Duke.

He should have let others
Take some of the strain,
By shrewd delegation
To share in the pain.

But the drum beat of history
Grows faint with each year,
And nothing seems quite
As it once did appear.

Thus it's easy to criticise
And re-fight each fight,
And play with toy soldiers
Till late in the night.

But nothing can dampen
Old Wellington's flame.
He was one in a million
And he played the great game.

As an icon of England,
He will always stand tall.
Arthur Wellesley – the Duke
Was the king of them all

23

THE HORSES

With chestnut* flanks gleaming,
And necks flecked with sweat,
Nostrils flaring and snorting,
Not a sight to forget.

The fetlocks and withers,
The haunch and the head,
God's most beautiful creature
'Twas often heard said.

And when dressed for battle
In fine leather tack,
They would canter and gallop,
Proud men on their back.

'Neath blistering sunshine
And harsh winter chills,
Over acres of wilderness
And rugged foothills.

Manes flying like ribbons
And long sweeping tails,
They were four-legged battleships
Without canvas sails.

But dragoons needed chargers
That were never bred slim,
They were heavy with muscle,
Sound in heart, wind and limb.

* Although most cavalry horses were black, as the Peninsular War progressed, replacement mounts were of various colours.

Lighter mounts were required
For reconnaissance needs,
Carriage horses or hunters
Were Hussars chosen steeds.

Thus thousands were needed,
And thousands were slain,
An equestrian graveyard
In the cauldron of Spain.

To feed them and groom them
And ride them to hell,
Was the job of the cavalry,
And they did it damn well.

Horses died short of forage,
Succumbed to disease,
Were killed by the cannon,
Cut down cruelly like trees.

But when we reflect
On the role that they played
In Wellington's triumphs,
This claim can be made.

Those great English horses,
Drawn from shires far and wide,
Are a source now accepted,
Of legitimate pride.

Although short in numbers,
As Wellington claimed,
The horses themselves now
Could hardly be blamed.

For Wellington too
Was a horseman of note,
Riding tall in the saddle,
A figure remote.

He needed a mount
Of exceptional skill,
With the heart of a lion,
Strong legs and strong will.

The one he selected,
'Copenhagen' by name,
Was a powerful charger
Who acquired national fame.

He served our great hero
In battle-torn Spain,
Survived cannon and musket,
Exhaustion and pain.

Now buried in 'Stratfield'*
By a gnarled old oak tree,
With a fine granite headstone
For pilgrims to see.

All the horses of England
Have a place in our hearts,
Whether carrying soldiers
Or pulling farm carts.

These fine loyal creatures
Deserve a salute,
As much part of history
As Wellington's boot.

* Stratfield Saye in Hampshire, Duke of Wellington's country estate.

24

MADRID
'Vivi les Angoles'

The beat of distant marching feet,
And wind-borne bugle calls
Come wafting through embrasures,
And across tall city walls.

The British are approaching,
With standards flying high,
Madrid their destination,
'Liberation' is their cry.

The counterfeit, King Joseph,
Disturbed from guilty sleep,
Soon quits his gilded palace,
To Valencia he will creep.

Escorted by an entourage,
And several thousand carts,
All piled high with plunder,
Fine wine, rare Spanish art.

This brother of Napoleon,
With his hollow claim to fame,
Could scarcely have become a king,
Without his famous name.

Thus Joseph Bonaparte retreats,
With quite indecent haste,
His spell as Emperor of Spain
Has now been laid to waste.

And on this bright, warm August day,
On every square and street,
The citizens pour from their homes,
The British troops to meet.

Church bells ring out with sonorous peals,
Palm branches by the score,
And olive leaves and tapestry,
Appear at every door.

Young Spanish girls with dazzling smiles
And frilled fiesta dresses,
Dance in the street without restraint,
Carnations in their tresses.

The carnival continues
Till later on that night,
When giant waxen candles
Provide a welcome light.

Amidst these celebrations,
And freely flowing wine,
The soldiers are quite overwhelmed
By compliments sublime.

To kiss a pretty girl or two
Is surely not a chore,
And bone-tired soldiers in red coats
Swap kisses by the score.

But not all kisses are divine,
As Private Wheeler* wrote,
He had a hairy Spanish man
Poke a tongue half-down his throat.

* The letters of Private Wheeler

Exuberance or gratitude,
You may call it what you will,
But Englishmen find such display
Less than a welcome thrill.

Poor Wheeler found it hideous,
And noted with disgust,
'This Spaniard's breath was garlicky
And he smelled of snuff and dust.'

Lord Wellington was fêted too
By crowds of eager girls,
All anxious to embrace him
And touch his manly curls.

They even begged a fragment
Of his dusty old frock coat,
So they could keep a souvenir
Of that hero so remote.

Thereafter in the city,
Triumphant he would ride,
In a mule-drawn landau
With young beauties by his side.

And still the Spanish showered him
With honours and awards,
They made him 'Generalissimo'
And gave him jewelled swords.

They granted him a great estate
Near Granada in the south,
And if they'd been permitted to,
They'd've stuffed rubies in his mouth.

While back at home in England,
The politicians chattered,
Should Wellington be promoted?
Was the issue now that mattered.

To create him a field-marshal,
Might make some others jealous,
Thus spoke the stiff-necked Duke of York
Whose hostility was zealous.

This rank would follow later
With medals, gifts and fame,
But now the shrewd Prince Regent
Added 'Marquess' to his name.

He was also offered money,
One hundred thousand pounds,
So that Wellington could now acquire
An estate with spacious grounds.

Majestic though this prospect was,
With coolness it was treated,
For there was bloody work afoot
Till Napoleon was defeated.

25

NAPOLEON

The dream is dead, the vision dashed
And glory turned to ashes,
As in his royal coach he sits,
Still dressed in silk and sashes.

Yet once like a colossus,
He straddled half the globe,
And many fearful nations
Were content to kiss his robe.

The Saxons and Bavarians,
Wurttenburgers and the Poles,
All felt he was invincible
And would achieve his goals.

But now his hopes are vanquished,
His lust for power, his schemes
Are nothing more than fantasies,
A broken man's sad dreams.

Lord Wellington, his enemy
And victor on the field,
Once said of him, that Caesar
Might have been compelled to yield.

His presence on the battlefield,
Worth forty thousand men?
But now this ruined Emperor,
Could scarcely muster ten.

The coachwheels begin turning,
They pass a blasted tree,
Where a wounded young French officer,
Murmurs 'C'est la vie'.

26

PARIS

From the streets of Monmartre
To the Rue de la Paix,
By the Seine's noble bridges
Parisians play.

Amid bustle and glitter,
The city's at peace.
For the first time in decades
All combat has ceased.

There's laughter and dancing
And candle lit balls,
In the low peasant's cottage
And nobleman's halls.

Will peace last forever?
Is Europe now one?
Can the French and the English
Relax in the sun?

The omens are cheerful.
The prognosis is clear.
There will be no more fighting
For many a year.

In order to demonstrate
Faith and good will,
The Bourbon King Louis
Has picked up his quill.

He has ordered his servants,
His maids and his cook,
To prepare a reception
For Arthur the Duke.

The Elysée is ready
The chandeliers glow,
And powdered French footmen
Line up in a row.

On fine polished marble,
By mirrors of gold,
A dozen French marshals
Stand steady – but cold.

Wellington enters,
The King by his side,
An orchestra strikes up
With strong Gallic pride.

But the be-ribboned marshals
In unison turn
Their backs to the Duke,
His presence to spurn.

With their tassels and sashes
And black shiny boots,
The marshals make Louis
Blush clear to his roots.

'I'm sorry,' says Louis
As he turns to His Grace,
'For the generals' impertinence,
Here – in this place.'

''Tis no matter, Your Majesty,'
Wellington sighs,
For their *backs* are familiar,
More so than their eyes.

27

LAST MEMORIES

Dusk falls on an English field,
As tawny owls start hooting,
And an old man at the village gate,
Imagines he hears shooting.

But it's a dream, a fantasy,
That echoes in his head,
His thoughts are many leagues away
With comrades long since dead.

He'll join them soon, of this he's sure,
He knows his life is over,
And then his tired body too
Will lie beneath the clover.

He walks back through the stillness,
To his cottage by the river,
And as he does, a sudden wind
Makes this ancient fellow shiver.

And once inside, he lights a lamp,
And sits down in a chair,
The flickering flame that lights the room
Illuminates his hair.

It's sparse and white in that gentle light,
No more a golden mane,
As it once was – so long ago,
On the burning hills of Spain.

His comrades all lie buried there,
Their white bones turned to dust,
The buttons on their uniforms
Dissolved by years of rust.

But he's kept his – all shiny bright,
And stored them in a tin.
He takes them out occasionally,
As he sips his home-made gin.

The memories come flooding back,
As he prods them with his finger,
Of daring deeds and prancing steeds,
The images still linger.

He's also kept his tunic safe,
His coat of British red,
But no soul will inherit it
When finally he's dead.

He's all alone and cannot share
His tales of blood and glory,
No wife, no son, no relative
To listen to his story.

It happened many years ago,
So long he can't remember,
Were they toiling 'neath the Spanish sun
In April or September?

What was the cause? Why were they there?
This poses a conundrum.
But truth to tell he knows damn well
The reason's far from humdrum.

For they all served their Sovereign King,
And took old George's shilling,
Though some were pressed to join and fight,
Many others were quite willing.

And still he feels a jolt of pride,
For serving on his country's side,
What better epitaph to write,
As he'll soon face eternal night.

He'll rest his bones on English soil,
After a life of sweat and toil,
And when he's gone, let angels sing,
His service was a noble thing.